Hugh Granville Tilley

N. C. House of Representatives 1887 & 1889

Teresa A. Johnson

Hugh Granville Tilley

Copyright © 2013 by Teresa A. Johnson

ISBN 978-0-9722724-9-0

Published for the author by
Blackfoot Burkino Cherokee Publishing
BBC Publishing
P.O. Box 58074 * Houston, Texas 77258
Phone: 832.504.1331
bbcpublishing@carolina.rr.com

My Great Great Grandfather
Hugh Granville Tilley
Served Two Terms in the

North Carolina House of Representatives
This book is dedicated to My Aunt,
His Great Granddaughter,
Tommie Fredricka Mitchell Ingram

Prologue

"My Great Grandfather, Hugh Granville Tilley, served as a member of the North Carolina General Assembly House of Representatives."

With those words, Tommie Fredricka "Isky" Ingram started a personal journey of discovery. This book provides a brief biography of North Carolina State Legislator Reverend Hugh Granville Tilley and captures events in the late 1800s that shaped his life, including his activities and accomplishments as a member of the North Carolina General Assembly in 1887 and 1889. It includes information from census reports that reveal important episodes in his life, such as education, relocation, and reinvention. It also explores how he is nurtured in a tolerant, blended North Carolina County of that era. Although Hugh Granville Tilley died young, he left his mark as a successful Farmer, a Conservationist, a Community Leader, a Politician, a Laborer, a Teacher, and a Minister.

Aunt Isky's Memory

Driving up to Aunt Isky's beautiful home, I commit to memory the remarkable beauty of her private residence. Aunt Isky taught school for more than twenty years in the Charlotte Mecklenburg School system. The builder of her home esteemed educators he requested she complete the interior construction and external landscaping. The sweat equity allowed her to secure her new home. With her sister, her brother-in-law and other family members their initiative help to build this home. Her brother-in-law Otto Johnson and his wife Geraldine Johnson Aunt Isky's sister obtained construction skills from Lee Roy Kirksey a Tuskegee Airman who built their home addition from the ground up. Lee Roy Kirksey and Otto Johnson installed flooring, framing, sheet rock, carpet, bathroom fixtures and cabinets, lighting fixtures, appliances, windows and doors in his home addition. Aunt Isky's home was in good hands. Aunt Isky's most stunning home built by our family with love became the place to hear a magnificent oral history lesson on Hugh Granville Tilley.

My Aunt Isky opened the front door on a beautiful fall morning day in 2002 and began to share an outstanding story. We bond with one-another at her kitchen table to drink a sunshine cup of coffee from yellow mugs before I traveled to work. It was our secret! Others in family were unaware we shared these mornings with one another. We both place our two cups of coffee down on the table and sit down on the chairs in her bay window nook area. Aunt Isky's mouth opened and these words came from her mouth "my Great Grandfather, Hugh Granville Tilley, was a member of the North Carolina House of Representatives (North Carolina General Assembly)." Suddenly on cue, while we take contentment in our coffee, rays of sunshine literally appeared through the window at her kitchen table. Her Great Grandfather, Hugh Granville Tilley my Great Great Grandfather, Hugh Granville Tilley is a part of North Carolina's post American Civil War history. It is impossible to imagine never hearing this history. We both sat quietly in her kitchen. We both gaze out the window then around the room. My mind sought for memories about People of Color in North Carolina's politics in the 1800s. We agreed there were topics on how the North along with the South fought during the American Civil War, specifically focusing on the abolition of slavery in the South and the South lobbying to afford new territories the right to introduce slavery upon their admittance into the union. Fundamentally we agreed limited information exists in the curriculum about life for people of color at this time. My Aunt Isky actually shatters an impression on life in North Carolina after the Civil War up to the early 1900s. Aunt Isky taught school for more than twenty years at West Charlotte High School. In November 2002 she planted a seed of hope in a sea of despair. Aunt Isky's inspirational account of our family's oral history and her courage while battling cancer inspires a quest to locate as much information as possible about Hugh Granville Tilley's life story. I am mesmerized actually unsure how I will drive to the University of North Carolina – Charlotte campus as an Adjunct Professor. This is a pivotal moment beginning a journey as a genealogical researcher.

Table of Contents

Chapter 1

Growing up in North Carolina

In the United States (U. S.) of America, between the 34o and 36o parallels, resides the state of North Carolina, which acquired its name from King Charles II of England (Province of Carolina). The family name "Tilly" originates from Belgian Johann Tserclaes (Count of Tilly). In the 1700s, the Tilly family immigrated to North Carolina from England and settled in Orange County, North Carolina, near the Little and Flat Rivers, once a part of Granville County. They were descendants from the Highlands of Scotland, Moravia, Germany, and Belgium. The family engaged in fox hunting, a British tradition. The shout of "Tally Ho" announced to hunters an opportunity to kill a fox. Relatives in this area kept hounds in pens in their backyard that they used for hunting. Hugh Granville Tilley grew up to eventually represent the Tally Ho Township, Granville County, in the 1887 and 1889 North Carolina General Assembly House of Representatives.

Cartographic Map

The U. S. Congress chartered the U.S. Army Corps of Engineers. They used the 1860 census to create a human cartographic map, the U.S. Coast Survey, showed that Orange County contained a small percentage of slaves. This small percentage indicated there were many free black residents in Orange County at the time of the census. Marcus "Mark" Tilly, Hugh Granville Tilley's father changes his last name in the census. In the 1850, 1860, and 1870 U. S. Census the recordation by the collector for Marcus "Mark" Tilley's race is the letter "W-White." In the 1880 U. S. Census the collector uses the letter "M-Mullato." The "Mullato" term gives a picture of a person of mixed race classification with the reflection of physical appearance and proportion of non-European features (see figure 1).

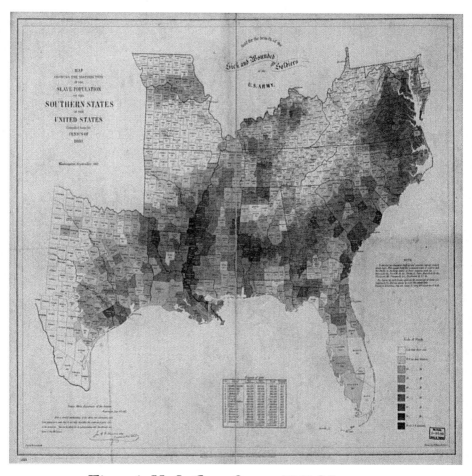

Figure 1: U. S. Coast Survey 1860 Map

Marcus Tilley, Hugh Granville Tilley's father, was born in Stem, North Carolina. Marcus Tilley owned a 300-acre farm in Orange County. This farm can be seen in this 1887 North Carolina map (see figure 2).

Figure 2: 1887 Map (Courtesy Duke Rare Book & Manuscript Collection)

The farm acreage represented considerable wealth for this era. This home is currently on the National Historical Landmark Registry for residential homes. On the Tilley farm they cultivated peas, beans, wheat, oats, rice, Irish potatoes, sweet potatoes, Indian corn, flax, flaxseed, tobacco, and hay and made butter. The farm also had fruit, nut, and hardwood trees. They made their own soap, lard, candles, rugs, quilts and clothing. They owned a horse, swine, milch cow and other cattle. They preserved meat, canned fruits and vegetables, and baked fresh bread. They fed their salaried workers a supper meal. However, simple farm life working in the fields slipped away in April 1861 when the U. S. American Civil War began. In May 1861, the state of North Carolina seceded from the Union. Hugh Granville Tilley was born in November 1861 seven months after the American Civil War began. Tilley was born to a free father in a slave state.

Undoubtedly the aftermath of the American Civil War and other events influenced his life. His education over the next two decades reflected a social consciousness within his family, the county, and possibly across the state. Hugh Granville Tilley grew up witnessing wars, black migration, immigration, imperialism, child labor discussions, families divided, and an industrial revolution.

His life experiences in this blended community uniquely prepared him for a legacy that is alive today. Appendix 1 provides a timeline of life-changing events.

Chapter 2

Education

Hugh Granville Tilley's father encouraged his son to pursue an academic education that extended further than the traditional basic education. His father understood the former slave state's culture. The winds of change brought hope with Hugh Granville Tilley's birth. The 1880 census shows Hugh Granville Tilley "At School." He was about twenty years old and probably aware that education opens doors as he masters Reading (phonics, spelling), Language, Drawing, Arithmetic/Math, Geography, Science, Penmanship/Spencerian Script and History. During the period of 1870-1890, the predominant age of college students was between seventeen and twenty-one years. In fact, for some prominent families it was an obligation at this age to afford their children the opportunity to travel to Europe to study. Teachers during this era attended two or four additional years after they completed basic school. Hugh Granville Tilley matriculated the equivalent of a college/divinity degree. He becomes a teacher and a minister. It's postulated that he taught school upon graduation. A typical school day for his students (Black, Mulatto, and Native American/Indigenous) would have begun at 9:00 am with oral reading, memorization, figuring on slates, mental arithmetic, a spelling bee, geography history and penmanship, ending at 1:30pm. As a result of public school bills introduced to help Native American/Indigenous People upon his election to the legislature, it is proposed that North Carolina State Representative Hugh Granville Tilley hoped to improve this community's wellbeing.

Figure 3: Hugh Granville Tilley
North Carolina House of Representatives 1887 & 1889

During this time education was not equitable. He witnessed the Native American "Termination" policy and the harshness of its implementation. "Termination" ranged in meaning from the death to the spirit, death to the body, death to the culture or death to the tribe. Given an opportunity to improve their educational and economic opportunities, he championed appropriations to change the lives of Native American/Indigenous people.

Chapter 3

Steps to the State Legislature

In 1861, a small minority of North Carolina men joined the Union Army; however a larger number of the state's men joined the Confederate States of America Army during the American Civil War. Yet during the war proof via congressional records exist that Republicans worked together with Democrats at the national level. Members of Congress negotiated to rebuild the U.S. after the war ends (Reconstruction-1865). Immediately after the end of the war, the nation attempted to recover, as families reconnected, people sought jobs, and the North and South struggled to rebuild mutual trust. Based on Hugh Granville Tilley's choices he became aware of the importance, the connection and the relevance between education, commerce, legislation and the struggles to reconstruct North Carolina after the war ends. When Hugh Granville Tilley was sent away to school, he studies the North Carolina legislative process and kept up with current events. The Legislative Branch includes the

Senate, and the House of Representatives, typically a 50-member Senate and a 120-member House of Representatives composes these two houses. The Laws, Statutes and Appropriations generated in 1887 and 1889 by the North Carolina General Assembly had far reaching impact, which is still felt today.

The members of the Republican and Democratic parties at the state level worked well together (excerpts of approved legislature can be found in Appendix 2, which provides insight to the appropriation of pension for windows, state-support to education, orphanages, funding veterans' benefits for soldiers and the protection of rivers and streams.) Appendix 3 provides a roster for both sessions of the legislature (1887 & 1889).

Visionaries and their impact

In the late 1800s the nation embraced the Industrial Revolution, a vision impacting communities across America. On the legislative front significant amendments were made to the nation's Constitution. Hugh Granville Tilley was just three years old when the 14th Amendment to the Constitution passed. North Carolina ratified the 14th Amendment two years later. The 15th Amendment, ratified in 1870, provided the right to vote. These guaranteed his rights as a full citizen of the U. S. of America, he was seven. Hugh Granville Tilley was a visionary who learns the land, to hunt fish and keep his feet in multiple cultures. State Legislator Tilley was a creative thinker so he respected an unchartered future and was aware of other visionaries across the nation. Each unique road he walked is geographically tied to a southern value system. The southern value system debates politics, government appropriations, racial divide, post-war recovery, commerce, transportation, agriculture, conservation, education, and labor. These concepts imprint in his brain a need to protect North Carolina's citizens and resources. Hugh Granville Tilley mirrors famous men (Congressman Henry Plummer Cheatham, Congressman Edward O'Hare, and Congressman George Henry White) from his community who serve the North Carolina Republican Party in Congress on agriculture and conservation.

Life Changing Events

The year 1886 proves to be dynamic with multiple personal life changing events for Hugh Granville Tilley. Hugh Granville Tilley's credentials make him sought after for advice. He is described as being articulate, proper, tall, statuesque and fair-skinned with curly hair. Hugh Granville Tilley marries Dema Green a full-blooded Native American/Indigenous woman. Dema Green is a member of his mother's tribe. Moma Dema, as she was affectionately called, never spoke of her family or her heritage. The "Termination" policy in America is punitive during this period in history. Congress passed multiple acts to gather Native Americans and place them on reservations, to stop viewing their land as a separate country, and revised tribal land ownership regulations. Hugh Granville Tilley's name links him to Granville County. Hugh Granville Tilley's sister, "Christanna" is his mother's quiet link to her culture. Fort Christanna became a place for trading and eventually comprised several Native Americans tribes – Haliwa-Saponi, Tutelo, Occaneechi, Eno, and Tuscarora. Moma Dema is depicted in family oral history as having beautiful long black hair down her back, very piercing eyes, and she rarely smiled. Through-out history, it's been said that members of the Indigenous People community would be killed (terminated) if they admitted they were a member of a tribe. During the 1800s, the termination policy to Mama Dema could have meant death, heritage loss or death to her spirit. To the government officials, the intent was to avoid responsibility for American Indigenous people.

In the latter half of 1886, there was an election in Granville County; Hugh Granville Tilley was elected to the State legislature. (See Figure 4) An affidavit written by Sheriff James Cereson in 1886 reads:

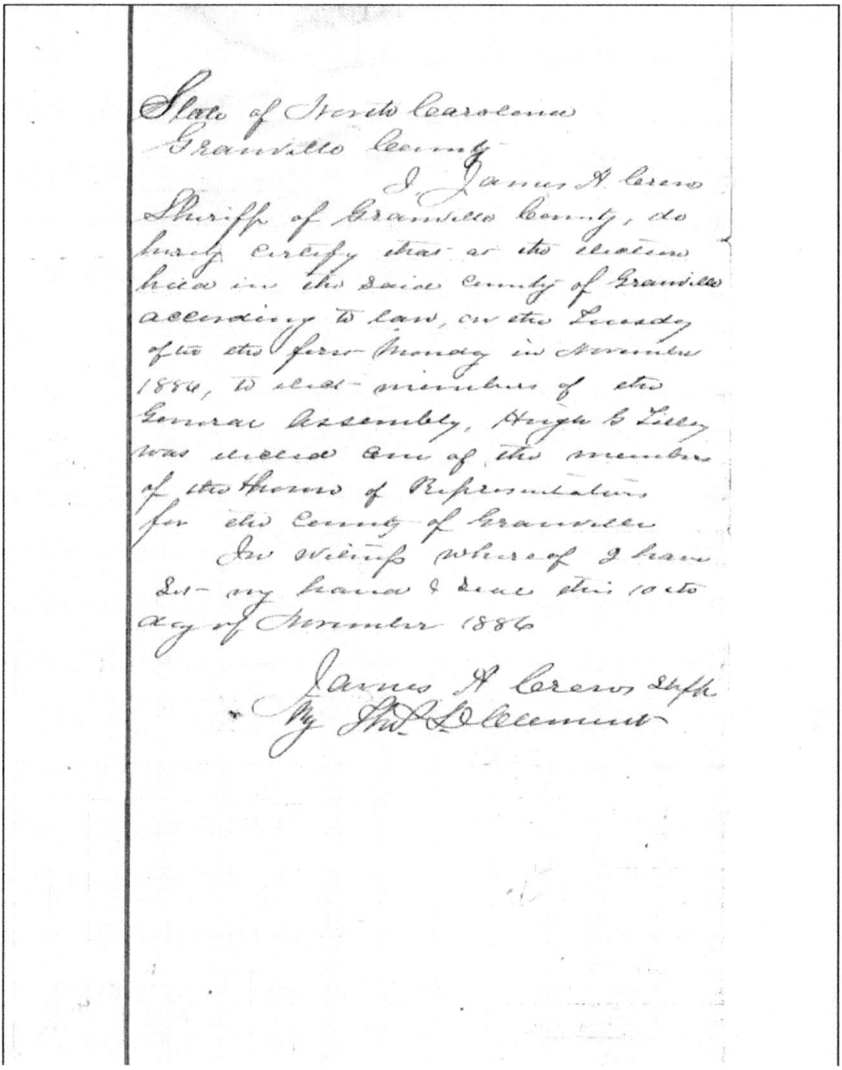

State of North Carolina
Granville County
I, James A. Crews Sheriff of Granville County, do hereby certify that at the election held in the said County of Granville according to law, on the Tuesday after the first Monday in November 1886, to elect members of the General Assembly, Hugh C Lilly was elected one of the members of the House of Representatives for the County of Granville
In witness whereof I have set my hand & seal this 10th day of November 1886
James A Crews Shff
By Thos L Clement

Figure 4: Notarized Nomination

It is important to note that, two years later, he won a second term to represent Granville County in 1889. He served two terms in Reconstruction politics in the state of North Carolina.

Reverend Hugh Granville Tilley's father Marcus "Mark" Tilley died in 1886. It became the responsibility of Hugh Granville Tilley not his older brothers, responsibility to care for minors and execute/distribute possessions of the estate in 1886. (See Figures 5-8)

Number 203.

ADMINISTRATOR'S OATH.—Printed and for sale at Harrell's Printing House, Weldon, N. C.

STATE OF NORTH CAROLINA, SS. IN THE SUPERIOR COURT.

Granville COUNTY.

I Hugh G. Tilley, do solemnly swear (or affirm) that I believe that Mark Tilley died without leaving any last will and testament: and that I will well and truly administer all and singular, the goods and chattels, rights and credits of the said Mark Tilley and a true and perfect inventory thereof return as provided by law; and all other duties appertaining to the charge reposed in me, I will faithfully and honestly perform with the best of my skill and ability. So help me God.

Sworn and subscribed before me this day of March 188-7.

H. G. Tilley

W. Lassiter Clerk Superior Court.

Figure 5: Administrator's Oath

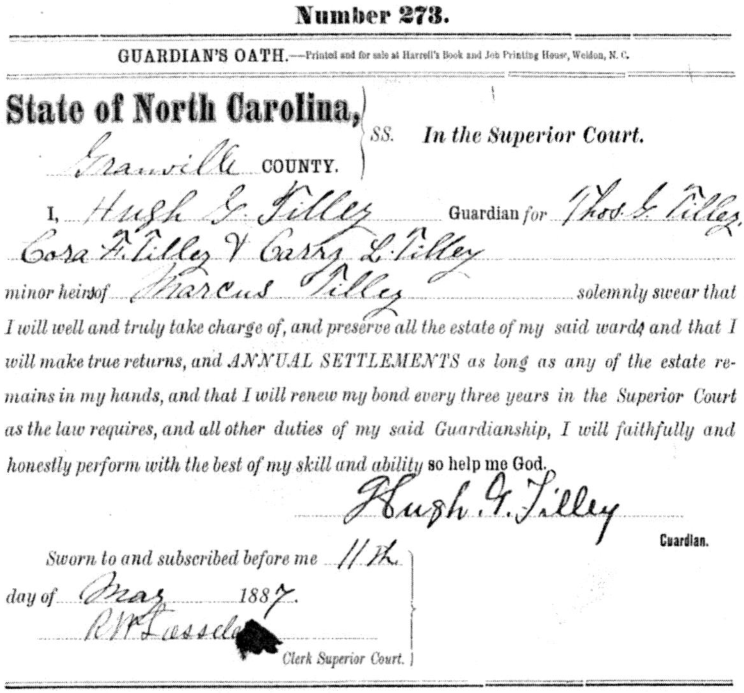

GUARDIAN'S OATH.—Printed and for sale at Harrell's Book and Job Printing House, Weldon, N. C.

State of North Carolina,

Granville COUNTY. } *SS.* **In the Superior Court.**

I, *Hugh G. Tilley* Guardian for *Thos G. Tilley,*
Cora F. Tilley & Carry L. Tilley
minor heirs of *Marcus Tilley* solemnly swear that
I will well and truly take charge of, and preserve all the estate of my said wards, and that I
will make true returns, and *ANNUAL SETTLEMENTS* as long as any of the estate re-
mains in my hands, and that I will renew my bond every three years in the Superior Court
as the law requires, and all other duties of my said Guardianship, I will faithfully and
honestly perform with the best of my skill and ability **so help me God.**

Hugh. G. Tilley
Guardian.

Sworn to and subscribed before me *11 th.* }
day of *May* 188*7.* }
R. W. Lassed. }
Clerk Superior Court. }

Figure 6: Guardian's Oath taken by Hugh Granville Tilley for
Marcus "Mark" Tilley's minors

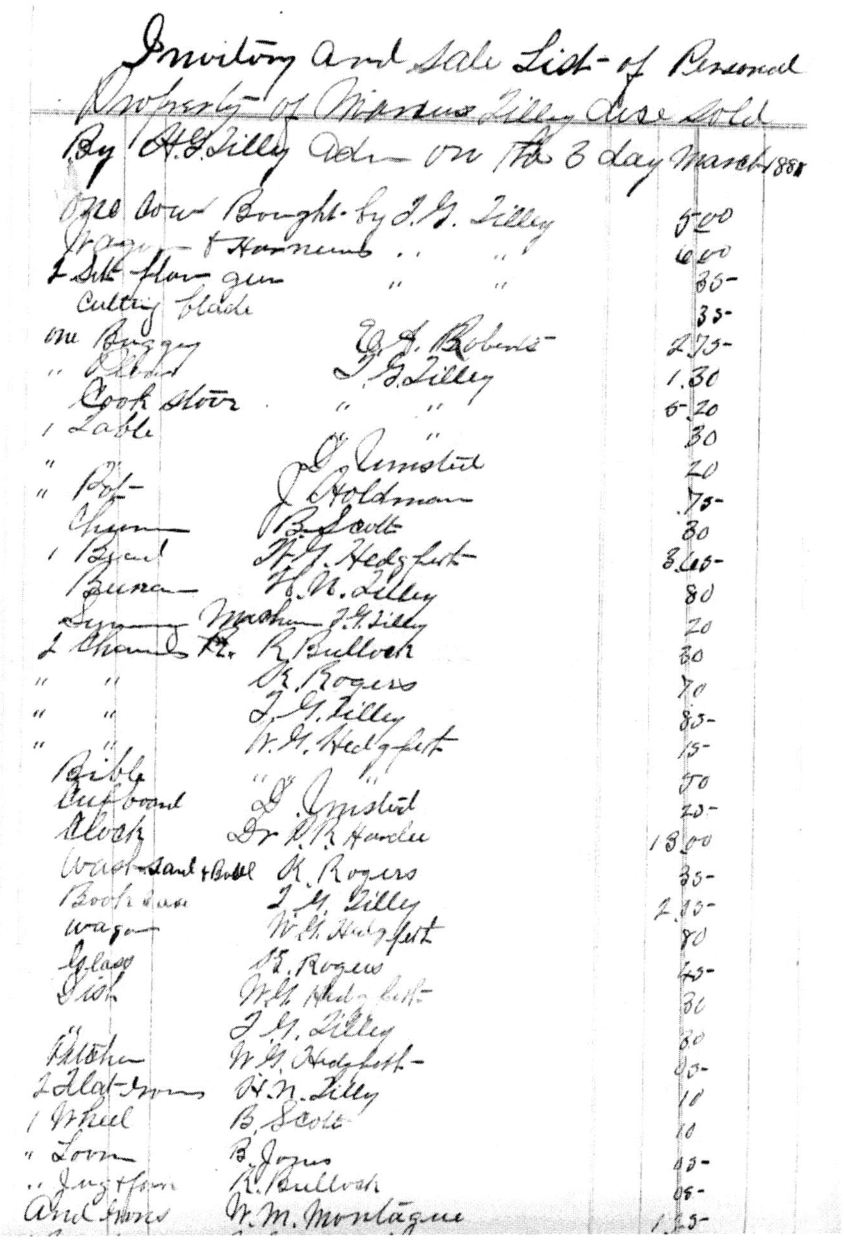
Invitory and Sale List of Personal
Property of Marcus Tilley Dise Sold
By H.G. Tilley Adm on the 3 day March 1881

One Cow	Bought by T.G. Tilley	5.00
Wagon & Harness	" "	6.00
1 Side flow gun	" "	35
Cutting blade		35
one Buggy	E.J. Roberts	2.75
" Plow	T.G. Tilley	1.30
Cook stove	" "	5.20
1 Table	"	30
"	D. Umstead	20
" Pot	J. Holdman	.75
Churn	B. Scott	30
1 Bed	W.G. Hedgpeth	3.65
Bureau	H.N. Tilley	80
Sewing Machine	T.G. Tilley	20
2 Chairs &c	R. Bullock	30
" "	K. Rogers	70
" "	T.G. Tilley	85
" "	W.G. Hedgpeth	15
Bible	" "	50
Cupboard	D. Umstead	20
Clock	Dr R.R. Hardee	18.00
Wash stand & bowl	K. Rogers	35
Book case	T.G. Tilley	2.85
Wagon	W.G. Hedgpeth	80
Glass	K. Rogers	45
Dish	W.G. Hedgpeth	30
"	T.G. Tilley	80
Pitcher	W.G. Hedgpeth	40
2 Flat irons	H.N. Tilley	10
1 Wheel	B. Scott	10
" Loom	B. Jones	05
" Jug & fan	R. Bullock	08
And Irons	W.M. Montague	1.25

Figure 7: Hugh Granville Tilley executor of Mark Tilley's life insurance, coffin, taxes, pg.1

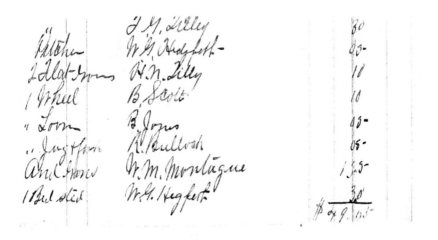

Figure 8: Hugh Granville Tilley executor of Mark Tilley's life insurance, coffin, taxes, pg.2

The next year starting was a common year of the Gregorian calendar, but truly it was an uncommon year in the life of Hugh Granville Tilley.

Chapter 4

Action to Reality

Hugh Granville Tilley decided to enter politics as a Granville County Republican with ambitions to create actionable, vital, sustaining engaging partnerships within the legislature.

Hugh Granville Tilley took the oath of office on January 5, 1887 in Raleigh, North Carolina from House Speaker John R. Webster in the North Carolina General Assembly. In 1887, he was approximately twenty six years old, a quarter of a century since the end of the American Civil War. From 1877 to 1887, he witnesses families whose fathers, husbands, and cousins were missing or dead. He witnessed children without protective adults. He was concerned about both white and black orphans without any support from the government. Grieving himself from the loss of a parent, he worked with other Republicans and Democrats to improve the state of

North Carolina's state-support to orphanages for children, both black and white.

Orphanage

In 1887, during North Carolina State Representative Hugh Granville Tilley's first term, his legislation incorporated an orphanage. It was located twenty-two miles north of Raleigh, North Carolina on Raleigh Road. The thought of an orphan home for non-white children was born in the church. Henry Plummer Cheatham, a future North Carolina Congressman, was a member of this original board for "The Colored Orphanage Asylum of North Carolina." Through oral history, it's told of how the entire community supported the Colored Orphanage by taking up Sunday school collections, and gathering clothing and food to help the children who lived in the orphanage.

Education

Hugh Granville Tilley worked to improve the state of North Carolina's educational appropriations. In the 1880s, America debated the role of child laborers and child labor laws. To North Carolina Legislators, the education of its citizens could usher in change. North Carolina Legislators advocated appropriations state-wide in 1887 to educate its people. It's evident that their appropriations manifest a philosophy that the more educated the people, the more cooperative they could become in their community. They asked why not change the mind of the average intelligence of the North Carolina population, thereby allowing a united North Carolina for all people to succeed.

Before the American Civil War, there were few institutions of higher education. Across the state, North Carolina State Representative Hugh Granville Tilley and his colleagues' championed securing funding to charter colleges and normal schools. The North Carolina General Assembly Session of 1887 incorporated or ratified amendments to charters for colleges of Asheboro Male & Female Academy, Asheville Academy, Beaufort High School Association, Biddle University (now Johnson C. Smith University), Central Institute for Young Ladies, Colored Orphanage Asylum (now Central Children's Home of NC, Inc.), Concord Female Academy, Kittrell

Industrial Normal School (African Methodist Episcopal Church Kittrell College), North Carolina State University, Leaksville High School. Closer to his wife's family part of state, the North Carolina General Assembly chartered the Croatan State Normal School (now University of North Carolina at Pembroke).

Infrastructure

Figure 9: Gull Shoal Lighthouse - Western Pamlico Sound, entrance to Pamlico River

Hugh Granville Tilley worked with fellow legislators to improve the economy by creating jobs and securing safety provisions on rivers for the state. (See Figure 9) The North Carolina General Assembly Session of 1887 successfully appealed to the fiftieth congress for safety appropriations for safe river navigation. The U.S. Congress responded to North Carolina's request. The US Army Corps of Engineers was the federal government's instrument to build coastal fortifications and postal offices, improve harbors, survey roads, eliminate navigational hazards on key rivers, build light houses and provide other national safety improvements. The Gull Shoal screw-piled light near the entrance to the Pamlico River became a reality to allow safe river navigation as a result of the funds appropriated by the U.S. Congress in response to the appeal of the North Carolina legislature. It's assumed that jobs were also created as a result of those federal appropriations.

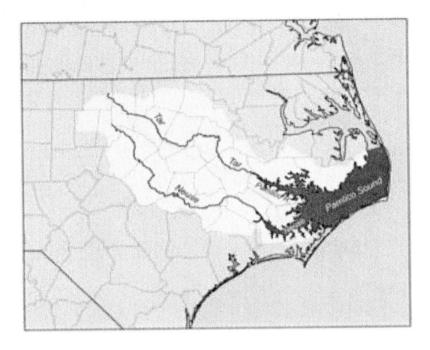

Figure 10: Pamlico Sound - Tar and Neuse Rivers

Conservation

Unfortunately, during this industrial revolution, the nation failed to focus on the management of land resources, especially in North Carolina.

North Carolina's original commerce, agriculture, expanded to include timbering. As America grew and expanded, a young nation's demands for hardwood trees increased. The demand for hardwood lumber for furniture, mines, settlements, schools, railroad construction, mills and other industries changed the North Carolina countryside. North Carolina's hardwoods of white cedars, red cedars, ash, birch, holly, chestnut, walnut, oaks, cottonwoods, and sycamore trees diminished.

However, the pollution in North Carolina's river effectively refuted any interest in preserving natural resources. The rivers become dark wastelands with dead animals and fish due to the logging industry. The timber milled to build the railroads and other commercial interest polluted the rivers and streams.

Hugh Granville Tilley worked to improve and protect the state of North Carolina's environment. The 1887 North Carolina General Assembly worked to improve awareness of the state's role

in the conservation of North Carolina's water resources. Felling timber, a method of harvesting hardwood trees, became a method for unsustainable commerce from 1870 to 1905. This session, of the North Carolina General Assembly passed legislation that made felling trees, in or otherwise obstructing streams and rivers, a misdemeanor for the White Oak River (Onslow County), Muddy Fork, Lower Little River (Alexander County), New Hope and N.E. Creek (Chatham County), Alaska (Alarka) Creek (Swain County), and Barnes Creek (Montgomery County). Throwing dead animals into the waterways became a misdemeanor in Walnut Creek (Wake County), Neuse River (Granville County), and Cashie River (Bertie County). The 1889 Legislature agreed that felling would only be allowed further than 20 m either side of a permanent stream. Across-the-board the consensus of this session enacted laws stating that felling must be scattered geo-graphically, designated habitat treaties must be left standing and trees and various barriers must be regenerated to prevent soil erosion.

North Carolina State Representative Hugh Granville Tilley valued the water resources that helped his community prosper and grow. He grew up on the Flat River, Little River, and Tar-Pamlico River Basin. Specifically these pure rivers enabled commerce, recreation, and fishing along the Tar, Eno, Flat, Little River and Neuse

Rivers. In Orange and Granville Counties several Siouan/Iroquois speaking tribes thrived on these rivers centuries ago.

Widows and Veterans

Hugh Granville Tilley worked with fellow legislators to appropriate pensions for widows and funded veteran's benefits for soldiers. The 1889 Compendium (Page 159 Chapter 198) reads

"an act for the relief of certain soldiers of the late war between the states annual pensions to be paid to certain soldiers and sailors injured in the war between the states and to certain widows to those totally incapacitated, $100, to those haven't lost leg above the knee or arm above elbow, $75, to those haven't lost foot, $50, to those haven't lost one eye or otherwise disabled and indigent whilst remaining unmarried, $25, certain persons excluded from the act."

Chapter 5

Integration and Segregation

The 1889 North Carolina General Assembly Session photograph appears to be segregated by race. The minority representatives are found in the lower half of the portrait in alphabetical order A.R. Bridges (#111 - Tarboro, Edgecombe Co.), Wilson Carey (#112 - Fitchie's Store, Caswell Co.), J. Holloway (#113 -Wilmington, New Hanover Co.), Valentine Howe (#114 - Wilmington, New Hanover Co.), John E. Hussey (#115 - New Bern, Craven Co.), A.R. Jacobs (#116 - Lawker, North Hampton Co.), D.R.H. Justice (#117 - Tarboro, Edgecombe Co.), N.R. Rawls (#118 - Garysburg, North Hampton Co.), Hugh Granville Tilley (#119 – Tally Ho, Granville Co.), R.C. Ward (#120 - Maven, Warren Co.), and James W. Watson (#121 - Henderson, Vance Co.). All whites are alphabetized by last name in the top of the portrait. (see Figure 13 and 14)

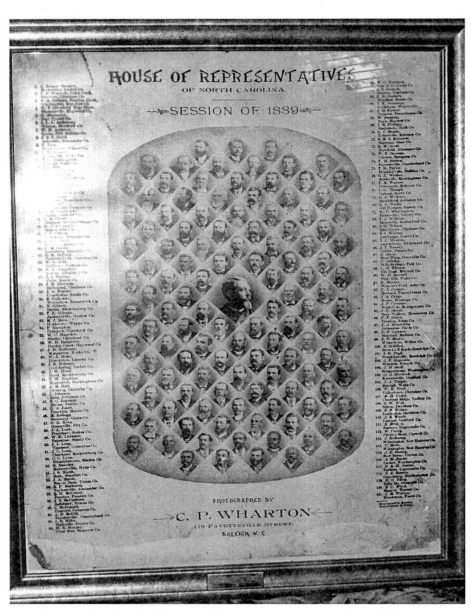

Figure 13: N. C. House of Representatives - Session 1889

32

Figure 14: Hugh Granville Tilley - #119

After the 1889 session for all intents and purposes this diversity, i.e., Blacks in North Carolina politics, decreased until the late 1960s. Black political power perceived as disruptive to social order yielded to terror and lynching. During this period racial segregation led to disfranchisement.

Chapter 6

Second District Mentors

North Carolina's 2nd Congressional District elected four Blacks to Congress during 1875 to 1901. The "Black Second" Congressional District included counties with a large minority population in close proximity to Granville County (Bertie, Craven, Jones, *Halifax,* Northampton, *Warren, Edgecombe,* Greene, Lenoir, *Vance*). Hugh Granville Tilley supported each of the four North Carolina Representatives to the U. S. Congress from the italicized counties while they served in Congress. The first Black to serve in the U. S. Congress from North Carolina was John Adams Hyman from Warren County (Roanoke River), 1875-1877. U.S. Congressman James Edward O'Hare from Halifax County (Cashie River), 1878-1880 and 1883-1887 was the second Black to represent North Carolina in the U. S. Congress. The third Black to serve in the U.S. Congress was Henry Plummer Cheatham from Vance County (Neuse River/New Hope River). Congressman Cheatham served on the Board of the first

"Colored Orphanage Asylum of North Carolina" approved by the 1887 N.C. General Assembly. The fourth Black to serve in the U.S. Congress was George Henry White from Tarboro Edgecombe County (Tar-Pamlico River Basin) 1896-1901. Note how each Congressman represented a county close to a major North Carolina river (Roanoke, Cashie, Neuse, Tar/Pamlico). The emphasis on rivers is a supporting hypothesis/connection that each of these members of Congress was a mentor to Hugh Granville Tilley. In the sessions that Hugh Granville Tilley served the Legislature, the Legislature protected the rivers these five men respected and chose to protect. In fact, many older boundaries in North Carolina used rivers and creeks as reference points to define their locations. The legislation approved in 1887 and 1889 directly related to his nurturing in the midst of the Tar River, Neuse River, Eno River and Flat River. Each Congressman had a direct link to these rivers. These water conservation efforts remain in effect to present day.

Relocation

North Carolina changed from the time of Hugh Granville Tilley's birth to just after his election to the N.C. General Assembly (House of Representatives) in 1887. The relative calm that exists today was impossible to imagine for people who were not of the majority culture (1890-1921). Upon completion of his term in the North Carolina General Assembly, it's clear Hugh Granville Tilley could foresee transformative winds of change blowing across North Carolina. Racial violence increased in North Carolina. His congressional mentors while he served in the legislature encouraged him to consider North Carolina's impossibility to differentiate its past from the present. Reverend Hugh Granville Tilley had the mental acumen and financial means to relocate his family to Washington, D.C. in 1890. He moved with his family into a row house near the U. S. Capitol Hill Complex on 625 Ackers North East (N.E.). He lived nine blocks from The Columbia Institution for the Instruction of the Deaf and Dumb, which is now Gallaudet University. Hugh Granville Tilley's Washington, D.C. cul-de-sac home was located in a community known for tolerance, education, jazz/blues music, and diversity in the late 1800s and early 1900s. While he lived in Washington, D.C., he worked for the North Carolina Republican Congressmen as a "Laborer" during the 51st Session of the U.S. Congress through the 57th Session of Congress. Hugh Granville Tilley resided in Washing-ton, D.C. approximately 10 years. In this northeast Capitol Hill neighborhood, positive influences were available to his young children. Capitol Hill inhabitants held positions in law, medicine, education, ministry, and federal employ-ees. In 1901 he moves a few doors down to 632 Ackers N.E. before returning to North Carolina in 1902.

Inopportunely the hero of the Rough Riders at San Juan Hill arrived in the nation's capital and similar to North Carolina this cities verve changes. Washington retreated from affairs of the south. The nation changed.

Chapter 7

Reinvention

After riding over many bumpy roads, Hugh Granville Tilley humbly walked on roads paved in success. He witnessed the establishment of colleges and normal schools, river navigation safety devices, an orphanage, and other visions he helped to became realities. There is no further mention that he continues in politics. Generally, hate had no place in State Representative Hugh Granville Tilley's life. Hugh Granville Tilley retired to a peaceful life as Farmer, Minister, Teacher and Grandparent in North Carolina. Twenty years after his return to North Carolina he lives in anonymity in the county that issues his death certificate. In fact the Informant for the death certificate barely has the ability to properly spell State Representative Reverend Hugh Granville Tilley's profession. The death certificate reads "Preachin" instead of "Pastor." (see figure 15)

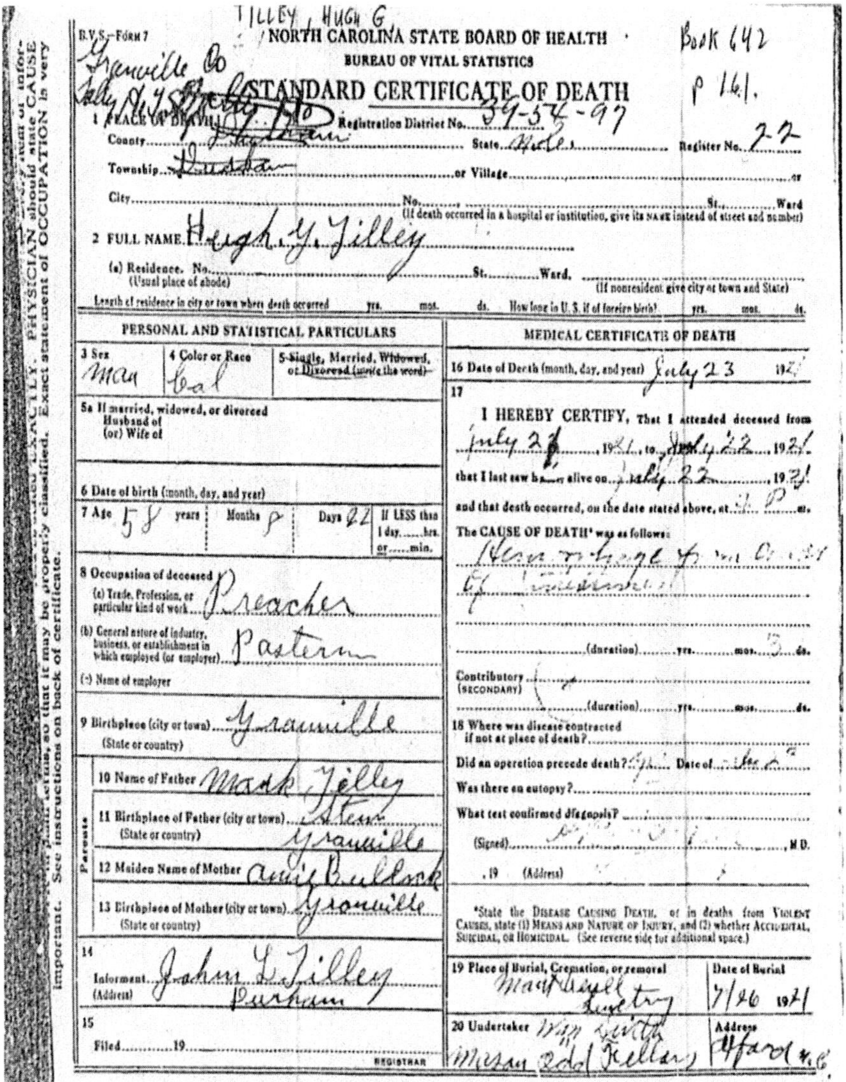
TILLEY, HUGH G.

B.V.S.—FORM 7

NORTH CAROLINA STATE BOARD OF HEALTH

BUREAU OF VITAL STATISTICS

STANDARD CERTIFICATE OF DEATH

Book 642

P 161.

Granville Co

1 PLACE OF DEATH Registration District No. 39-54-97

County ... State ... Register No. 22

Township ... or Village ... or

City ... No. ... St. ... Ward (If death occurred in a hospital or institution, give its NAME instead of street and number)

2 FULL NAME Hugh G. Tilley

(a) Residence. No. ... St. ... Ward. (Usual place of abode) (If nonresident give city or town and State)

Length of residence in city or town where death occurred yrs. mos. ds. How long in U. S. if of foreign birth? yrs. mos. ds.

PERSONAL AND STATISTICAL PARTICULARS

3 Sex Man

4 Color or Race Col

5 Single, Married, Widowed, or Divorced (write the word)

5a If married, widowed, or divorced Husband of (or) Wife of

6 Date of birth (month, day, and year)

7 Age 58 years Months 8 Days 22 If LESS than 1 day ... hrs. or ... min.

8 Occupation of deceased (a) Trade, Profession, or particular kind of work Preacher

(b) General nature of industry, business, or establishment in which employed (or employer) Pastor

(c) Name of employer

9 Birthplace (city or town) Granville (State or country)

10 Name of Father Mark Tilley

11 Birthplace of Father (city or town) (State or country) Granville

12 Maiden Name of Mother Annie Bullock

13 Birthplace of Mother (city or town) (State or country) Granville

14 Informant John L. Tilley (Address) Durham

15 Filed ... 19 ... REGISTRAR

MEDICAL CERTIFICATE OF DEATH

16 Date of Death (month, day, and year) July 23 1921

17 I HEREBY CERTIFY, That I attended deceased from July 21 1921, to July 22 1921

that I last saw h... alive on July 22 1921

and that death occurred, on the date stated above, at ... m.

The CAUSE OF DEATH* was as follows:

(duration) ... yrs. ... mos. 3 ds.

Contributory (SECONDARY)

(duration) ... yrs. ... mos. ... ds.

18 Where was disease contracted if not at place of death?

Did an operation precede death? ... Date of ...

Was there an autopsy?

What test confirmed diagnosis?

(Signed) ... M.D.

, 19 (Address)

*State the DISEASE CAUSING DEATH, or in deaths from VIOLENT CAUSES, state (1) MEANS AND NATURE OF INJURY, and (2) whether ACCIDENTAL, SUICIDAL, OR HOMICIDAL. (See reverse side for additional space.)

19 Place of Burial, Cremation, or removal — Date of Burial 7/26 1921

20 Undertaker — Address Oxford N.C.

Figure 15: State Legislator Hugh G. Tilley Death Certificate

State Representative died July 23, 1921 from a hemorrhage of the intestines. His nephew Reverend John L. Tilley, son of his brother Harvey Tilley, concurred as an informant on the death certificate. Harvey Tilley told his family that his brother, Hugh Granville Tilley, was a minister and teacher at Mt. Vernon Baptist Church. (See Figure 16 & 17) John L. Tilley is the grandson of Marcus "Mark" Tilley. John L. Tilley is the son of Harvey Tilley.

described as being diligent in business, a kind neighbor, genial, and friendly.

Their oldest daughter, Sennie married Joseph "Joe" Herbert Daniel (1897-1960) who was the son of John Henry Daniel (1865-1940) and Mary "Mollie" Booker Currin (1866-1936) in 1918. Three of their four children survived to adulthood, Josephine Lewis (1919-1993), Julian Miller (1922-1963) and Mary Lou (1927).

Joe and Sennie Daniel were the third and last of the Thomasson lineage to reside in the house at Water Line Farm. The 150-year-old landmark in the Tally-Ho community was struck by lightening June 8, 1982 and burned to the ground. *Submitted by: Vera Daniel Mangum, 1200 Julian Daniel Road, Stem, NC @27581-9670.*

464 PETERSON THORP, JR. AND JENNIE TAYLOR THORP

My mother, Jennie Taylor Thorp, (B. August 7, 1850 - D. September 26, 1909) was the daughter of Dr. William Thorp and Arabella Young.

Her mother died when she was three years old and she and her sister, Ella, lived at Goshen. When quite young, she went to Mrs. Veneable's Boarding School in Oxford and later to Nash and Kollochs in Hillsboro.

Her father was married the second time to Lucy O. Gregory. After that she stayed at home and visited the Coopers in Henderson, the Youngs in Oxford and relatives in Petersburg, Virginia.

She was married to her cousin, Peterson Thorp, Jr. on June 14, 1877. They had five children Belle Young, Henry Norman, Wesley Young, Lucy Jane, and Benjamin Person.

For a few years we had governess' to teach us. Then Belle went to Hilliard's School in Oxford; later to St. Mary's in Raleigh.

Henry ("Bargie" as he was called) went to Horner's in Oxford. He was doing well, but had to stop on account of his bleeding spells. All three of the boys had this trouble.

I am thankful to say that none of the grandchildren have inherited this trouble.

My mother was anxious for us all to have good education; especially for Belle and myself to study music, since she played the piano. I am sure she was responsible for my going to Salem.

I remember how very proud she was when she came to my graduating recital. Such a long, tiresome trip, but it was worth it.

She loved to read and sewed nicely. She was most unselfish, a loyal Episcopalian, and a devoted mother.

My father, Peterson Thorp, Jr., (B. November 30, 1839-D. December 6, 1908) was the son of Benjamin Person Thorp and Ann Eliza Norman who had six sons and three daughters.

He went to Mr. Hughes' Boarding School in Person County; later finished at Horner's School in Oxford.

He entered Chapel Hill expecting to study medicine. In his second year in college he had pneumonia and had to come home.

The Civil War had started and he enlisted in the 55th North Carolina Regiment. He is listed in Clark's History as a Hospital Steward. I have several letters written while he was in the service.

After the war he kept back and farmed a tract of land his father had given him, which I now own.

He came down to Oak Hill and opened a general country store and did real well.

In 1877, June 14, he married his first cousin Jennie Taylor Thorpe. They lived at Oak Hill until their family needed more room. Then at the Young Place for awhile. Back then to Oak Hill for the rest of his life.

He kept a few hounds and enjoyed fox hunting with Uncle Ben and Mr. George Daniel. He usually rode horseback except for going to Oxford or Stovall.

He was always interested in buying land, which was cheap then, and at the time of his death he owned 4300 acres.

I remember him as a perfect type of southern gentleman. Always wearing a stiff-bosomed white shirt, linen collar, and black string tie.

He was most highly respected and greatly loved by friends and neighbors far and near. A man anyone would be proud to claim as one's father. *Submitted by: Martha Morton, 5802 Tattersall Dr., Durham, NC 27713; grandniece of Mrs. Morton with permission from Elizabeth Thorp Morton, granddaughter of Mrs. Morton.*
Sources: Written by Lucy Jane Thorp Morton (1889-1980). (Mrs. John Gregory Morton, Sr.)

465 MORE THAN TWO CENTURIES OF BENJAMIN PERSON THORP

For the first time in 203 years, there is no Benjamin Person Thorp in the Thorp family with the passing of Benjamin Person Thorp, III on July 30, 1979. There has been a Benjamin Thorp in the Thorp family and Granville County for 203 years. They are all buried at Goshen, the family cemetery.

Benjamin Person Thorp, I married Jane Taylor. He was the son of Peterson and Martha (Patty) Person. His mother was General Thomas Person's sister of whom Person County is named. Born April 21, 1776; Died June 12, 1858.

His son, Benjamin Person Thorp, II, married Ann Eliza Norman. Born November 23, 1813; Died June 12, 1858.

His son, Benjamin Person Thorp, III never married. He fought in the Civil War and killed General Reynolds in the Battle of Gettysburg. Born September 8, 1844; Died December 28, 1914.

Benjamin Person Thorp, Sr. married Ida Jackson. He was the son of Peterson and Jennie Thorp Thorp. Born July 7, 1891; Died August 13, 1935.

Benjamin Person Thorp, Jr. married Leora Currin. He was the son of Benjamin Person Thorp, Sr. and Ida Jackson. He served in World War II. Born December 10, 1922; Died July 30, 1979.

Benjamin Person Thorp, III married Gina Evans. He was the son of Benjamin Person Thorp, Jr. and Leora Currin. Born January 18, 1948; Died July 30, 1979. *Submitted by: Martha E. Morton, daughter of Lucy Thorp Morton, 5802 Tattersall Drive, Durham, NC 27713.*
Source: Compiled in 1979 by Lucy Thorp Morton (Mrs. George D. Morton, Jr.)(1929-1999).

466 HARVEY N. TILLEY AND EMMA B. TILLEY

The 1900 Census lists Harvey N. Tilley and Emma B. Tilley in Tally Ho Township of Granville County. They had settled on Mountain Road east and south of Stem.

Harvey Tilley was the son of Marcus and Amy Bullock Tilley of the nearby Knapp of Reeds area. Emma was the daughter of Squire and Betsy Glenn of Rougemount in Person County.

Their children were John Lee, Addie Mae, Lillian Beatrice, George, Garland, Harvey, and Alice. According to their youngest daughter Alice, this is how her parents and other relatives had obtained their land "up in the mountains." During the War, "Pete" Reuben Bullock, Harvey Tilley's paternal grandfather saved Benjamin Bullock's money and silver by cleverly concealing them. He put them in a sack at bottom of the creek and marked them with a cattail broken in a way he'd recognize after the Union Army had passed.

The Tilleys were among the families that established a viable farming community and by the early 1870s organized Mt. Vernon Baptist Church out of Pine Grove Baptist Church.

The Mr. Vernon Church building also served as a school. At one time Harvey Tilley's brother, Rev. Hugh Tilley was the minister and teacher. Hugh Tilley later became a Representative in the North Carolina General Assembly. He dedicated much of his attention to establishing the colored orphanage in Oxford.

The Old Harvey and Emma Tilley Home Place.

The Tilley family lived and farmed in Stem until the WWII until the federal government designated that land as the site where it would build Camp Butner. The Tilleys and other families in the camp area had to sell their property and move.

The Tilley Family. Matriarch Emma B. Tilley and sons Garland, George, Rev. John L. and Harvey E. Tilley.

They relocated in Creedmoor in Brassfield Township. Again they helped establish a community. The congregation of Mt. Vernon Baptist Church dismantled and rebuilt the church building to a hilltop on Mt. Energy Road, now, Moss-Hayes Road. Tilley family members again held responsible positions. Alice Tilley was church clerk and George and Mack Tilley were trustees. Through the years family members served in such other capacities as teaching Sunday school, singing in the choir, ushering, directing the Christmas plays, and maintaining the church building. On the third Sunday in September 1942 Rev. John Lee Tilley, a former pastor of the church and Dean of the School of Religion at Shaw University, preached the dedication sermon. The church library was later named in his honor.

The Tilley Family. Matriarch Emma B. Tilley and daughters Lillian B. Moore Addie M. Jones and Alice E. Tilley; also daughter-in-law Phyllis Tilley.

Most of the grown children of Harvey and Emma Tilley remained in the Creedmoor-Butner area. John Lee was in Raleigh and later St. Augustine, Florida, and Harvey lived in New York City for many years before returning to North Carolina and settling in Oxford. *Submitted by Glennette Tilley Turner, 1541 Hill Avenue, Wheaton, IL 60187.*
Sources: 1870, 1880, 1900 Granville County Census and family interviews.

Figure 16: Harvey Tilley brother of Hugh Tilley

Granville County Heritage

North Carolina

Volume I

2002

Figure 17: Granville County Heritage

It is possible North Carolina Congressman George Henry White, who retired from congress to work in his family's under-taker business and led the Oxford Colored Orphanage in Granville County or members of the Odd Fellows, was entrusted with Hugh Granville Tilley's burial arrangement. Hugh Granville Tilley's relationship with Congressman George Henry White while living in Washington, D.C. enabled Demar Green Tilley the protection she needed in this time of sorrow. Hugh Granville Tilley's wife Dema Green Tilley died in 1957 at the age of 95 years old.

Hugh Granville Tilley's life choices helped his family, church, Granville County conservation, orphaned children, widows, and educational institutions for state-wide residents. State Representative Reverend Hugh Granville Tilley dedicated his life to the inhabitants of the state North Carolina.

Hugh Granville Tilley received the correct name "Hugh" which means charity, heart, and intelligent soul. His decades of accomplishment should also include in the meaning of his name: creative, courageous, compassionate, determined, forgiving, perseverant, and strong. Behavior is genetically passed from generation to generation. Hugh Granville Tilley's eyes had focus. He was a genius, fair, eloquent, dynamic, strong, kind, hardworking, a visionary.

Tommie Fredricka "Isky" Ingram, who was responsible for originating this investigative journey, died January 2003. She shattered an impression of life in North Carolina after the American Civil War. The Equanimity State Representative Reverend Hugh Granville Tilley conveyed in society prevails throughout our family. He was born and thrived despite multiple setbacks and events that weighed heavily on his daily existence. However the love, behavior, generosity, and unselfishness taught by Hugh Granville Tilley are alive in our family.

Appendix 1

Hugh Granville Tilley Timeline

1823	Hugh Granville Tilley's father born
	Marcus "Mark" Tilley (other sources born-1830)
1850-60s	U.S. policies towards Indigenous People –
	Termination
1861	Hugh Granville Tilley born November 1861
	Orange County
	Civil War begins 1861
	Abraham Lincoln President
1864	Hugh Granville Tilley's wife Demar Green Tilley
	born May 1864 - Nova Scotia
1865	Reconstruction Era begins
	Andrew Johnson President
1867	Tar Heel Republican Party
	(Mixed race political meeting)
1868	Black representation in the N.C. State Legislature
1869	Ulysses S. Grant President
1877	Rutherford B. Hayes President
1880	Census reports him "At School"
	Christanna Tilley Moore returns home
1881	James A. Garfield President
1885	Grover S. Cleveland President
1886	Certified as Granville County winner

	State Representative
	N.C. House of Representative November 10, 1886
	Marries Dema Greene
	Father dies
1887	Sworn in January 5, 1887 - N.C. General Assembly
	Incorporates or Amends multiple schools across
	the state
1888	Walter A. Tilley born November 1888
1889	Re-elected Granville County State Representative
	N.C. House of Representative
	Mt. Vernon Baptist Church Minister
	Charters Kittrell College & Biddle University
	Benjamin Harrison President
1890	Relocates family to Washington, D.C.
1893	Grover S. Cleveland President
1895	Pauline Tilley born November 1895
1897	William McKinley President
1898	Julia Tilley born November 1898
	Democrats over throw elected Republican
	government
1901	Theodore Roosevelt President
1909	William Taft President
~1910	Walter Tilley changes name
1913	Woodrow Wilson President
1921	Hugh Granville Tilley dies July 23, 1921
	Warren G. Harding President

Hugh Granville Tilley

1957   Demar Green Tilley dies October 25, 1957

Appendix 2

LAWS AND RESOLUTIONS

OF THE

State of North Carolina,

PASSED BY THE

GENERAL ASSEMBLY

AT ITS

SESSION OF 1887,

BEGUN AND HELD IN THE CITY OF RALEIGH

ON WEDNESDAY, THE FIFTH DAY OF JANUARY, A. D. 1887,

WHICH ARE PREFIXED

A REGISTER OF STATE OFFICERS, JUDICIARY, A LIST OF COM-
MISSIONERS OF AFFIDAVITS, MEMBERS OF THE GEN-
ERAL ASSEMBLY, AND STATE CONSTITUTION.

LI HED BY U H RITY.

RALEIGH:
OSEPHUS DANIELS, State Printer and Binder.
1887.

Excerpts - 1887 & 1889

1887- Granville County

Incorporation of the Colored Orphan Asylum of North Carolina

Section 1810 amended marriage between Indians and Negros void. Application only to Croatan Indians

Mecklenburg road law repealed as to Granville County

Chapter 47.

An act to incorporate the Colored Orphan Asylum of North Carolina.

Whereas, It has been deemed expedient to establish in the county of Granville, state of North Carolina, an asylum for the care and maintenance, and mental, moral and industrial training and education of the colored orphan children in the state aforesaid; and whereas, it is desired that the said asylum shall be incorporated by the general assembly of North Carolina; therefore,

The General Assembly of North Carolina do enact:

Section 1. That chapter A. Shepherd, J. Perry, W. A. Patillo, M.C. Ransom, Henry Hester, H. P. Cheatham, I. Alston, O. Bullock, A. B. Fleming, J.W. Levy, J. C. Jeffreys, J. T. Reynolds, M. F. Thornton and H.E. Long and their associates and successors, be and they are hereby created a body politic and corporate, under the name and style of the "Colored Orphan Asylum of North Carolina," with power to receive, purchase and hold property, real and personal, not to exceed one hundred thousand dollars, to sue and be sued, to plead and be impleaded, to contract and be contracted with, and to do all other acts which may be necessary to manage the business of the corporation herein created and to carry out the intent and object thereof, provided the same shall not be inconsistent with the laws of North Carolina.

Sec. 2. That the said corporation shall have power to choose from the corporators named in this act, or from such as may be associated with them hereafter, a board of directors, to consist of such number as may be deemed advisable, who when chose and duly organized by the election of a president and secretary, shall have power to make all necessary by-laws and regulations for the convenient and efficient management and control of the affairs of said corporation, and to appoint such number of trustees as the said directors may deem expedient, who shall when appointed perform such duties as may be assigned to them by the said board of directors. The said trustees shall be subject to removal at the pleasure of said board of directors.

Sec. 3. That the object of said corporation shall be to receive, maintain and care for such colored orphan children of the state of North Carolina as under the laws and regulations of said corporation may be deem practicable and expedient, and to impart to them such mental, moral and industrial education and training as may fit them for usefulness in life.

Sec.4. That the said corporation shall have power to secure the control of such orphans by the written consent of those nearest of kin to them, or of those having the control of the said orphans, or by petition for such control when necessary to the superior court clerk of the county in which said orphans may be domiciled, who may in his discretion grant such control to said corporation; and it shall not be lawful for any person or persons to in any way interfere with said corporation in the management of said orphans after they shall have been entered and received by the aforesaid corporation.

Sec. 5. That the said corporation shall have power to discharge any of said children from the asylum when it shall be deemed advisable by such authority as shall be designated by the board of directors aforesaid.

Sec. 6. That the location of the said asylum shall be at or near Ox-ford, Granville County, North Carolina.

Sec. 7. This act shall be in force and after its ratification.

In the general assembly read three times, ratified the 28th day of February A.D. 1887.

Chapter 198.

An act for the relief of certain soldiers of the late war between the states annual pensions to be paid to certain soldiers and sailors injured in the war between the states and to certain widows

(Page 159 Chapter 198) an act for the relief of certain soldiers of the late war between the states annual pensions to be paid to certain soldiers and sailors injured in the war between the states and to certain widows to those totally incapacitated $100 to those haven't lost leg above the knee or arm above elbow $75 to those haven't lost foot or hate in $50 to those haven't lost one eye or otherwise disabled and indigent whilst remaining unmarried $25 certain persons excluded from the act

Chapter 254.

An act to amend section one thousand eight hundred and ten of The Code.

The General Assembly of North Carolina do enact:

Section 1. That section one thousand eight hundred and ten of The Code of North Carolina be amended by adding thereto the words: "That all marriages between an Indian and a Negro or between an Indian and a person of Negro descent to the third generation inclusive shall be utterly void: Provided, this act shall only apply to the Croatan Indians.

Sec. 2. That this act shall be in force from and after ratification.

In the general assembly read three times, ratified the 7th day of March A.D. 1887.

Chapter 344.

An act to repeal chapter one hundred and seventy-two of the laws of one thousand eight hundred and eight-five, known as the Mecklenburg road law, for Granville County.

The General Assembly of North Carolina do enact:

Section 1. That chapter one hundred and seventy-two of the laws of one thousand eight hundred and eight-five, known as the Mecklenburg road law, so far as it refers to Granville County, be and the same is hereby repealed.

Sec. 2. That the road fund in said county shall be applied to the payment of general county expenses.

Sec. 3. This act shall be in force from and after its ratification.

In the general assembly read three times, ratified the 7th day of March A.D. 1887.

Session of 1887 – Resolutions

Whereas, there are comparatively few stations of the life-saving service and signal service on our North Carolina coast, and whereas, these stations are a great protection to human life and to commerce; therefore,

Resolved by the House of Representatives, the Senate concurring; That our members of the house of representatives of the congress of the United States be and they are hereby requested to use every exertion in their power to obtain appropriations from congress of the United States for and the establishment of life-saving service and signal service on our North Carolina coast. That a copy of this resolution be mailed by the secretary of state to each of our senators and representatives in congress. Ratified this the date of January, A.D. 1887.

Fiftieth Congress - Appropriation

Excerpt(s) from the Fiftieth Congress Sess. I

Chapter 1113 An act providing for the establishment of a life-saving station at the harbor of Kewaunee, Wisconsin, and at other places herein named. Be it enacted by the Senate and House of Representatives of the United States of America in Congress assembled, That the Secretary of the Treasury be and he is hereby, authorized to establish additional life-saving stations upon the sea coast of the United States as follows: ... two between Ocracoke Island and Cape Lookout, North Carolina.

Chapter 1221.

An act for the establishment of a light house and fog-signal at or near Gull Shoal, Pamlico Sound North Carolina be it enacted by the Senate and House of Representatives of the United States of America in Congress assembled, That a light-house and fog signal be established at or near Gull Shoal Pamlico Sound, North

Carolina, at a cost not to exceed 30,000 dollars Approved October 19, 1888.

Chapter 1220.

An act for establishing a light off Pamlico Point, North Carolina. Be it enacted by the Senate and House of Representatives of the United States of America in Congress assembled, That a screw-pile light house be established on the shoal at or near Pamlico Point, entrance to Pamlico River, Pamlico Sound in North Carolina at a cost not exceeding twenty-five thousand dollars, to replace the present light on the shore at Pamlico Point. Approved October 19, 1888.

Excerpt from the Fifty-first Congress Session II Chs 907

Because of Chapter 907 multiple river improvements in the Session I 1890 Cheat River, Cape Fear, Contenia Creek, Water Route, Currotuck Sound Norfolk, Neuse River, New River, Pamlico and Tar River, Trent River, Lumber River, Roanoke River, Yadkin River Ocracoke

Inlet Mackey's Creek North East (Cape Fear) River, Water Way New River, Fishing Creek, Pasquotank River.

Excerpt(s) from the Fifty-Second Congress Sess. I Chs. 351, 352 1892

Chapter 352.

An act relating to the limitation of hours of daily service of laborers and mechanics employed upon the public works of the United States and the District of Columbia. Be it enacted..., that the service and employment of all laborers and mechanics who are now or may hereafter be employed by the Government of the United States, by the District of Columbia or by any contractors or subcontractors upon any of the public works of the United States or of the said District of Columbia is hereby limited and restricted to eight hours in any one calendar day, and it shall be unlawful for any officer of the United States Government or the District of Columbia or any such contractor or subcontractor whose duty it shall be to employ, direct or control the services of such laborers or mechanics to require or permit any such laborer or mechanic to work more than eight hours in any calendar day except in case of extraordinary emergency. Approved August 1, 1892.

1889-Index-Granville County

Time of holding superior court changed

Unlawful to fell timber in waters of Granville County and fail to remove in five days (Misdemeanor)

Relating to roads and highways in,

Penalty for using dynamite to destroy fish

Multiple universities chartered, funded

For Croatan Indians, Robeson county

Chapter 114.

An act to prevent the felling of timber in the streams of Granville county.

The General Assembly of North Carolina do enact:

Section 1. That it shall be unlawful for any person to fell any timber, brush or other obstructions in any of the streams of Granville county on which there are mills, or across which there are bridges, and allow the same to remain in said streams more than five days.

Sec. 2. That any person violating this act shall be guilty of misdemeanor and upon conviction shall be fined not less than five nor more than fifty dollars.

Sec. 3. That this act shall be in force from and after this ratification.

Ratified the 14th day of February A.D. 1889.

Appendix 3

Black and White members appear to have worked together well in the North Carolina Legislature – General Assembly – House of Representatives 1887 and 1889

x   MEMBERS OF THE GENERAL ASSEMBLY.

HOUSE OF REPRESENTATIVES.

JOHN R. WEBSTER, Rockingham County, Speaker, Reidsville.

NAMES OF MEMBERS.	POST-OFFICE.	COUNTY.
ABELL, E. S	Smithfield	Johnston.
ALLMAN, W. N	Franklin	Macon.
ASHCRAFT, C. A	Beaver Dam	Union.
BEASON, N. W	Abbott's Creek	Davidson.
BELL, E. R	Giddensville	Sampson.
BENNETT, D. N	Norwood	Stanly.
BINGHAM, THOMAS	McBride's Mills	Watauga.
BLEVINS, RILEY	Weaver's Ford	Ashe.
BLOUNT, E. C	Willow-Green	Pitt.
BROODEN, C. H	Goldsboro	Wayne.
CANDLER, J. M	Webster	Jackson.
CHAPPELL, JOSHUA	Bostick's Mills	Richmond.
CHEEK, J. A	Hillsboro	Orange.
CHERRY, M. C. S	Bethel	Pitt.
CHILLCUTT, B. H	Brown's Summit	Guilford.
COFFEY, D. D	Collettsville	Caldwell.
COPELAND, ELIHU	Belvidere	Chowan.
CRAWFORD, W. T	Waynesville	Haywood.
CRAWFORD, G. W	Marion	McDowell.
CRENSHAW, R. C	Whitakers	Edgecombe.
CRISP, JOS. L	Snowah	Graham.
CROOM, R. M	Burgaw	Pender.
DOUGHTON, R. A	Sparta	Alleghany.
DAVIS, J. M	Grissom	Granville.
DEAVER, J. F	Deavers	Transylvania.
DORSETT, W. M	Hookerton	Greene.
ELLIS, W. J	Ellaville	Davie.
EVANS, A. V	Manteo	Dare.
EWART, H. G	Hendersonville	Henderson.
FARMER, W. W	Wilson	Wilson.
FRANKLIN, S. C	Mt. Airy	Surry.
FULTON, R. P	Columbia	Tyrrell.
FRIES, H. E	Salem	Forsyth.
GATLING, RIDDICK	Gatlington	Gates.
GRAY, M. A	Kinston	Lenoir.
GREEN, F. F	Trenton	Jones.
HALSTEAD, J. W	Lilly	Camden.
HAMPTON, PIERCE	Currituck C. H.	Currituck.
HARRINGTON, T. W	Harrington	Harnett.
HAYES, A. H	Charleston	Swain.
HINTON, P. A	Rose Dale	Pasquotank.
HOLLOWAY, JOHN	Wilmington	New Hanover.
HOLMAN, J. B	Cool Springs	Iredell.
HOLT, T. M	Haw River	Alamance.
HOOVER, C. W	Raleigh	Wake.
HOWE, VALENTINE	Wilmington	New Hanover.
HULL, M. F	Mulgrove	Catawba.
HUSSEY, J. E	Newbern	Craven.
JORDAN, ALLEN	Troy	Montgomery.

N. C. House of Representatives – 1887 Session – pg 1

HOUSE OF REPRESENTATIVES—*Continued.*

NAMES OF MEMBERS.	POST–OFFICE.	COUNTY.
KELL, J. T	Harrison	Mecklenburg.
KING, H. E	Peanut	Onslow.
LAZAR, A	Mooresville	Iredell.
LINDSEY, W. R	Madison	Rockingham.
LONG, J. W	Concord	Cabarrus.
LYON, C. C	Elizabethtown	Bladen.
MACON, NAT. H	Louisburg	Franklin.
MANGUM, J. S	Pernell	Wake.
MANNING, J. W	Dymond City	Martin.
MARTIN, J. B	Arapahoe	Pamlico.
MEARES, A. C	Pireway	Columbus.
MILLS, J. C	Brindletown	Burke.
MOORE, J. W	Huntersville	Mecklenburg.
MORGAN, H. C	Columbus	Polk.
McCLURE, W. H	Hayesville	Clay.
McKINNON, D. C	Big Oak	Moore.
McMILLAN, H. C	Red Springs	Robeson.
NEWSOM, J. C	Five Oaks	Stokes
OAKLEY, T. C	Durham	Durham.
OSBORNE, E. K. P	Charlotte	Mecklenburg.
OVERMAN, L. S	Salisbury	Rowan.
PARHAM, J. A	Lockville	Chatham.
PARSONS, W. L	Wadesboro	Anson.
PASCHALL, J. T	Siler City	Chatham.
PATTON, W. O	Murphy	Cherokee.
PEARSON, RICHMOND	Ashville	Buncombe.
PERSON, J. B	Fremont	Wayne.
PINNIX, J. C	Longtown	Yadkin.
PITTMAN, J. M	Halifax	Halifax.
PRITCHARD, J. C	Ray	Madison.
PRITCHETT, J. A	Greensboro	Guilford.
PROCTOR, F. H	Denver	Lincoln.
RAWLS, N. R	Garysburg	Northampton.
REDDING, T. J	Caraway	Randolph.
REGAN, D. C	Lumberton	Robeson.
SANDERS, JOHN	Glenmore	Johnston.
SHARP, J. J	Sharpsburg	Nash.
SHAW, JOHN G	Fayetteville	Cumberland.
SCHENCK, H. F	Shelby	Cleveland.
SNELL, C. W	Mackey's Ferry	Washington.
SNIPES, E. T	Murfreesboro	Hertford
SORRELL, P. A	Cary	Wake.
SOUTHERLAND, J. D	Kenansville	Duplin.
SPELLAR, T. R	Windsor	Bertie.
STANCILL, R. H	Margarettsville	Northampton.
STEVENS, W. E	Clinton	Sampson.
STEWART, GEO. C	Green's Grove	Rutherford.
SUTTON, T. H	Fayetteville	Cumberland.
S ARATT, J. G	Jackson's Hill	Davidson.
SWAIN, S. P	Smithville	Brunswick.
EMPIE, J. A	Raleigh	Wake.

N. C. House of Representatives – 1887 Session – pg 2

HOUSE OF REPRESENTATIVES—*Continued.*

NAMES OF MEMBERS.	POST-OFFICE.	COUNTY.
THOMAS, C. R. Jr	Beaufort	Carteret.
TILLEY, H. G.	Tally Ho	Granville.
TURNER, S. J	Bakersville	Mitchell.
WARD, R. C	Warrenton	Warren.
WATSON, I. B.	Engelhard	Hyde.
WATSON, J. M	Henderson	Vance.
WATERS, B. W	Washington	Beaufort.
WATTS, R	Taylorsville	Alexander.
WEBSTER, W. P.	Yanceyville	Caswell.
WELLS, L. N	Leicester	Buncombe.
WHITE, J. A	Scotland Neck	Halifax.
WHITE, E. A	Belvidere	Perquimans.
WILLIAMS, J	Burnsville	Yancey.
WILLIAMSON, J. H	Louisburg	Franklin.
WILSON, J. F	Crowder's Creek	Gaston.
WIMBERLY, D.	Tarboro	Edgecom .
WOODY, J. F	Bethel Hill	Person.
WORTH, J. M	Worthville	Randolph.
YORK, TYRE	Trap Hill	Wilkes.

N. C. House of Representatives — 1887 Session — pg 3

House of Representatives

Speaker, Augustus Leazar, Iredell
Clerk, Thomas B. Womack, Chatham

Representative	County	Representative	County
Elbert W. Scott	Alamance	Shade L. Wooten	Lenoir
Robert F. Robinson	Alexander	William A. Hoke	Lincoln
Rufus A. Doughton	Alleghany	William H. Blaxton	McDowell
John J. Dunlap	Anson	George A. Jones	Macon
Riley Blayton	Ashe	D. F. Lawson	Madison
John S. Nazah	Beaufort	J. B. Cofield	Martin
Edward E. Outlaw	Bertie	N. Gohlen	Mecklenburg
C. C. Lyon	Bladen	J. W. Houd	Mecklenburg
Rufus Galloway	Brunswick	James C. Long	Mecklenburg
James S. T. Baird	Buncombe	Luke M. Bmeer	Mitchell
Melvin B. Carter	Buncombe	J. F. Crowder	Montgomery
John H. Hoffman	Burke	M. J. Blue	Moore
Charles McDonald	Caldwell	J. H. Phillips	Nash
William C. Newland	Caldwell	John Holloway	New Hanover
E. M. DeFord	Camden	Valentine Howe	New Hanover
A. H. Chadwick	Carteret	A. R. Jacobs	Northampton
Wilson Carey	Caswell	Edward E. Rawls	Northampton
A. M. Hiatt	Catawba	T. E. Gilman	Onslow
John M. Edwards	Chatham	Thomas M. Cheek	Orange
S. G. Wilson	Chatham	B. D. McCotter	Pamlico
William R. Trull	Cherokee	E. J. Burn	Pasquotank
Ivary A. Boyd, Jr.	Chowan	Robert C. Johnson	Pender
J. A. Bell	Clay	John D. Peebles	Perquimans
W. C. Hamrick	Cleveland	J. T. Yancey	Person
John J. Lonar	Columbus	M. C. S. Cherry	Pitt
John E. Hussey	Craven	George S. King	Pitt
Archibald D. McGill	Cumberland	Grayson Arledge	Polk
Thomas H. Sutton	Cumberland	Benjamin Stillkin	Randolph
Pierce Hamilton	Currituck	J. H. Pugh	Randolph
S. M. B. Sullivans	Dare	T. J. Wooten	Richmond
R. M. Wall	Davidson	T. D. Ragan	Robeson
Ezekiel V. Walser	Davidson	R. M. Walters	Robeson
John A. Hendricks	Davie	Thomas W. Hopkins	Rockingham
John B. Miller, Sr.	Franklin	G. T. Walker	Rockingham
John T. Nichols	Durham	James S. McCubbins	Rowan
Edward Brokaw	Edgecombe	T. M. Wilson	Rutherford
Daniel Justice	Edgecombe	William B. Murphy	Sampson
John T. Reynolds	Forsyth	W. E. Stephens	Sampson
John T. Clifton	Franklin	W. K. Littleton	Stanly
Charles M. Cooke	Franklin	James A. Leak	Stokes
Robert A. White	Gaston	L. C. Waugh	Surry
Martin Kellogg	Gates	J. A. Franks	Swain
Robert Carver	Graham	T. N. Cooper	Transylvania
Rufus Amis	Granville	David Alexander	Tyrrell
R. G. Tilley	Granville	James A. Marsh	Union
Noah B. Broadus	Greene	James H. Watson	Vance
Ogden A. Starbuck	Guilford	R. C. Ward	Warren
James B. Woods	Guilford	Levi H. Branson	Wake
W. H. Anthony	Halifax	Eugene C. Beddingfield	Wake
Thomas H. Taylor	Halifax	W. H. Bennett	Wake
William Pearson	Harnett	James A. Temple	Wake
W. H. Hargrove	Haywood	J. H. Snell	Washington
John G. Grimm	Henderson	J. A. Crisp	Watauga
James L. Anderson	Hertford	Matthew J. Hare	Wayne
Mehrah Makely	Hyde	John K. Overman, Jr.	Wayne
John B. Holman	Iredell	Edward O. Martin	Wilkes
Augustus Leazar	Iredell	Nathan Bass	Wilson
W. A. Bills	Jackson	M. H. Vestal	Yadkin
Josephus Johnson	Johnston	W. P. Whittington	Yancey
E. A. Wellons	Johnston		
F. M. Freear	Jones		
Franklin F. Green	Jones		

N. C. House of Representatives — 1889 Session

Appendix 4

Family Tree for Hugh Granville Tilley including author - six generations

Family Tree for Hugh Granville Tilley
6 Generations

Marcus Tilley	Hugh Granville Tilley				
	Dema Greene Tilley	Julia Tilley Mitchell			
		John Mitchell	Thomas Mitchell		
				Thomas Mitchell Jr.	
			Laura Morgan Mitchell		
				Claudia Mitchell	
			Gladys Mitchell Bass		
			Hugh Mitchell	Geraldine Johnson	
			Eugene Mitchell		
			John Mitchell		
			Harvey Mitchell	Otto Johnson	
				Johnsonie Williams	
				Jesse Williams	
				Tommie Fredricka Ingram	
				J. Ingram	
				Carolyn Simms	
				P. Simms	

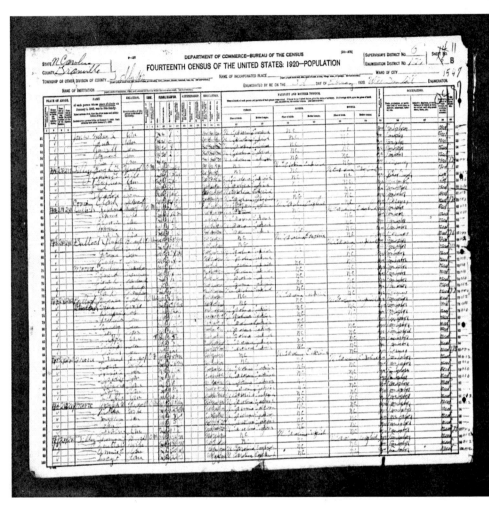

Census 1920

1860 Census

Marcus Tilley	Marcus Tilley
Mary	Elizabeth
Adolphus Tilley	Christanna Tilley
J. Norman Tilley	Hugh Granville Tilley
Ira E. Tilley	Harvey Tilley
Anna L. Tilley	Thomas Tilley
Alice L. Tilley	Decia Tilley
Roscoe Tilley	Cora Tilley
James Tilley	Cara Tilley

Thomas Mitchell, Gladys Mitchell Bass, Julia Tilley Mitchell, Harvey Mitchell

John Mitchell

Thomas Mitchell and Launa Mitchell Aunt Isky's Parents

Tommie Fredricka "Aunt Isky" Ingram, Chinyelu Williams, Ttosam Williams

Otto Johnson and Geraldine Mitchell Johnson

Teresa A. Johnson, Chinyelu Williams, Ttosam Williams, Dean Williams

Appendix 5

References

North Carolina State Archives, Raleigh, North Carolina
Census, Population of the US Granville County,
North Carolina Microfilm

Census, Slave Schedules of the US 1850-1860 Granville
County,North Carolina Microfilm

Census, Population of the US Orange County, N.C. Microfilm

Vital Records of North Carolina Birth, Death 1913 to present
N.C. State Board of Health and Vital Statistics, Raleigh, N.C.

Granville County Estate Records 1746-1919 – Estate papers,
unpublished of Granville County, N.C. Marcus Tilley
1887–177, filed at the N.C. Division of Archives and History,
Raleigh, N.C.

Granville County Sheriff Notarized petition certifying Hugh
G. Tilley's nomination to the N.C. House of Representatives
N.C. Division of Archives and History, Raleigh, N.C.
Books
White, Barnetta McGhee, A Quest for Enslaved Ancestors:

The Extended Family of Griffin Fountain of VA &
NC, Gateway Press, Inc. Baltimore, Maryland 2002

Granville County Heritage North Carolina Volume I 2002
number 466Congressional Record 55th Congress 1st Session
(26 January 1899) page 1125

Congressional Record 56th Congress 1st Session (5 April
1900) page 1814

Articles and Interviews
Ingram, Tommie Interview in Charlotte, North Carolina 2002

Internet
1. Map Showing the Distribution of the Slave Population of
    the Southern States Compiled from the Census of 1860
http://www.mappingthenation.com
2. The North Carolina State Library Archives
http://statelibrary.dcr.state.nc.us
3. North Carolina History Project - "Black Second"
http://www. northcarolinahistory.org
4. Black Americans in Congress – Henry Plummer Cheatham,
Representative from N.C.http://baic.house.gov/member-
profiles/profile.html?intlID=19
5. Black Americans in Congress – George Henry White,
Representative from N.C.http://baic.house.gov/member-

profiles/profile.html?intlID=22

Estate Papers

Marcus "Mark" Tilley Estate Paper Excerpts

(H. G. Tilley Executor)